SHADES OF RED: A POETIC LOVE STORY
BY: AUDREYANNA GARRETT

ISBN: 9781794235182

The Dedication

This book is dedicated to my greatest love, my best friend and the man who I deemed the mate to my soul- - thank you for your love. You are now and will be forever the best thing to ever happen to me. I cherish every moment spent with you. This is to a lifetime filled with memories of minutes of loving you...

SHADES OF RED:
THE PRELUDE

So
I give you
In shades
My story
A journey
In poetry
Not to be confused with
Shadows
Patchy dense
Or overcast areas,
It's
Not the same as
Shade thrown,
A colloquialism
That's
All to familiar
To some...

No.

My shades
Are not the same at all.

My journey encompasses
Real pain
Real joys
Real shame
In the most humble sense.

I
Forced she,
Her,

Me,
To remain in the light,
Out of darkness,
But
Somehow,
I'd still encounter them,
"The shadows"...

Somehow,
I'd walk into them.

Somehow,
My choices didn't steer me clear of them
So,
I had
No fear,
Of getting caught up
Or
Found on
My back side.

I refuse to hide
From the ride
So I
Give you
The light,
The dark,
And all hues in between...

I give you,
Shades of
Burgundy,

Crimson,
Blood orange,
Cardinal,
And
All others
Of the same
Family.

The colors that bleed
Are the same colors
That
Give just as much
Melancholy,
As pleasure,
In everything we see...

So,
I give
My feelings,
My emotions,
My pain,
My joys,
My world,
In the form of
Streams,
Gulfs,
Lakes,
Rivers,
And oceans of tears,
Joy
And all that it means
In life,

In
Love,
Success,
And defeat
To me.

I give you,
My
Poetic love story...

SHADES OF RED:
THE JOURNEY

It's so hard
To be
Me...

Everywhere
I turn,
Everyone I see
Trying to tear me down
With
An inexplicable ability
To,
"Understand" me.

I was
Trippin',
Slippin',
Until I began falling
On concrete slabs,
Where
I sustained scrapped knees,
Cut hands,
And
Bruised pride.

But I still
Didn't get off the ride...

You would have thought
Seeing shades of red,
Like fresh cuts
Bleeding,
That

I'd longed
For it to end,
All the hating,
The nagging,
And
The staring
But,
I accepted that
It may never cease
So
I had to find a way
To thrive
Exist
And be,
Regardless...

Pulsating
Sounds of pain,
I'd hear the beats
Of my own drum
And heart strings
Ripping
So vividly,
But positive thoughts still
Consumed me
Somehow.

So,
I got up
And
Moved forward,
With

Bandaid covered wounds
And scratches,
That ran through
My soul…

Tattered
From the road blocks endured,
All because knowing you
And
Loving you
Were
One of my life's
Greatest challenges.

I lost the war.

I had to heal
While broken.

I had to
Find peace
In loss.

I had to
Fight everyday
The urges
To return to you…

I could only view
Shades of darkness
Because
Nothing was visible.

I coped with it,
Because
Every attempt
To be with you
Was better than
Not having you
At all.

And
Even though
The visible images of pain are now gone,
It still feels real.

The hurt
I swear
I can still feel
The way I loved you,
And
The way we felt to
Be
Good.

Some part of me
Refused to
Release it,
After all for me
Broken,
Felt natural,
But,
I had to block it
From my present.

So,
I sent it away,
I tried to bury it,
In the darkest part of me.

Ironically,
Despite how I thought
I'd never see this day,
I sing
Now,
Songs of love,
Heart felt hymns,
And
Poetic words.
Only to later find
It was only
A temporary fix.

But,

You came
And loved me through
The tears I shed for him.
And although
I couldn't commit,
You deserved
Every ounce of me
I could give
But,
I gave
What was left
To him.

I possibly destroyed you…

I gave
All that I could spare
And
All that was left
Untouched
By you.

You made a place in my world.

We built a foundation,
A friendship,
That withstood all
Of his multiple attempts to return.

Even
His selfish claims
On my life.

But still I
Felt bad,
You had to endure questions,
And
Uncertainty
For my life choices,
Because
I knew,
When I found time to get better,
I'd give you
Every part of me

He broke.

Every part,
That
You so carefully restored...

Through you,
I began to see him
For what he was.

Nothing but pain
For me,
Melancholy,
Tears
And catastrophe!

I needed you,
But
I could no longer
Stomach the pain.

I didn't want the stress of you,
I couldn't be thoughtful
Of your pain and,
Still seek to love you,
One day.

Yet,

My heart
Still called your name,
Selfishly,

I wanted all of you
And him.

I wanted everything,
Even though I could only give
The least of me.

But,
I pressed on...

I had to see life
For what I was worth now
So,
I kept walking
One foot
Ahead of the other.

I was making progress
Until
Prompted by the unknown.

I took a sharp turn,
Down the wrong way,
Onto the block where
Heartbreak resides,
And
He was there.
And,
Your love was now clear,
In the distance...

I tried to hide

From this setback.
To scared to change course,
Still,
In the alley of shadows
Of past love,
Haunted,
I screamed
Loud,
Yet
Unheard.

Not even
The man who was healing me
Could carry me
Out of this.

I paused for a moment.

I desperately needed clarity.

A new strategy,
A
New approach,
I searched for new blockades,
I tried to tap into it,
Every inch of my being,
But fear,
Of the unknown
Brought back chills.

I screamed,
In hopes that he'd

Seek me.

I yelled for him
To come
And rescue me,
But,
No one answered the call...

Stifled,
I lay still
In the dark
Fearful,
Shades of
Raisin
And wine,
Dark and deep
And
I was surprisingly
Faithful!

Hoping
That he will,
One day,
Save me.
And you'd still,
Be there for me...

After all,
He,
Still fills this hollow heart of mine.

I was

Forced to admit this,
As I waited in vain.

I was forced to acknowledge
That I,
Was just buying time
Until his return...

Stuck on stupid,
Questioning,
Will it vanish?

That desire to hold on,
Because
It doesn't appear that I can,
Or will
Ever
Let go of
The unrequited love...

The memories,
Filled with heart songs,
A new beat,
Destiny,
Of undying passion,
A sultry melody,
We breath
In sync
Yet,
Burgundy ,
Is all
I see.

Deep agony,
Melancholy,
I'm consumed with
Begging him
Still
To
Help me...

I have no room
To breath,
So,
I fell to my knees
And
They were bare now,
Although
Recently healed
By the medicine of a dangerous
Temporary love.

A sexy,
Passionate man
Took my hand
It wasn't you.

It was something new
Now,
But worse,
It was
Toxic.

I flung to him for acceptance,

And
Love.
He wanted me
And I liked it,
Yet
You remained,
Unacknowledged,
And in some instances
Disrespected,
Not taken serious,
And in hindsight
I get it...

I couldn't see the good in you,
Too scared
To take a chance,
I had to go for what felt good,
But burned in the end.

Like fire,
In shades of brick and lava,
I saw his desire,
I didn't argue it,
But,
He just wasn't,
What I needed...

Yet again
I called to him
Over,
And over,
"Hey Lover"...

Looking back
Through remorseful eyes
You were right,
I was blinded by
Intimate moments.

So I now
Apologize.

I
Was left to question
Were they worth it?

They being tears,
The ones I shed...

Was it necessary?

The pain I felt,
Because I was now left
To ponder it,
For several moments,
To realize that
For me to deal with his imperfections,
Poor choices,
Bad logic,
And two faces,
Despite the warnings,
Is well,
Stupid!

I tried it again
Against my better judgment,
At least one more time,
But then
Once more
Became the last
Consciously.

I needed to
Free myself
From poor decisions.
I needed to
Rescue myself
From misdirected feelings.

But
It was no surprise that
He still couldn't see.

I went from living and loving horizontally
To falling
Vertically.

And I knew
It wasn't meant to be...

So,

I needed
To find new perspective.
And
Just like that

I needed new bandages.

Surprisingly,
Even though he was no good
He still
Affected me...

But,
Nothing would work
To keep the blood,
Which now seeps
In silhouette of lava,
From the wounds he left me.

It was
Burning through all,
Too hot,
Nothing could keep it from spilling over
Into the spaces of my broken world.

The cracks deepen,
Damaging everything,
Yet
I watch it
Drip...

Still in awe
I find some courage,
And some faith,
To pick up and press on,
To see how loving
Turned my judgement so wrong.

But
Still I tried,
For love
In other's arms,
Not yours.

I traveled away from the drums,
The beats of your heart
The music you made...

I had to find a new way
To understand what love was about,
So,
I found new energy.

I came to understand
That my pulse has it's own tune.

I needed to dance to it.

I needed it to be the only song I danced to,
For awhile at least...

And just like that,
While engulfed in the dance
Of my broken soul tunes,
I encountered you.

He,
The friend,
Brushed past my shoulder,

Butterflies flood back,
And I,
Too emotional
Due to recent trauma,
I
Was susceptible,
To manipulation,
Pain,
Hurt,
And the cycle
Of being broken...

For to be consumed with emotion
When typically emotionless
Is atrocious...

I could't decipher
His fake from your real
And
Well
It wasn't
Something I could deal with,
Without sleep,
For fear of bad decisions.

I was once again
Confused.

Just wanting and needing him
To be
The one...

Not ashamed of my struggle,
Bruised and broken,
Eyes now glisten,
Moistened with tears
And tattered,
I still remained
Humble...

And to my surprise,
He found love in my pain.
He too could relate
So
He took pride in my faith,
To love again.

He told me his story
And I knew then
We'd find love
After hurting so much...

We unconsciously
Learned to love one another
Through it all
So
It felt right.

He and I.

We felt like
Soul mates...

Like,

The feeling you get
When you kiss your best friend
For the first time,
Confused yet content...
But happy,
You're now free to express
Your attraction...

Something like that.

Because,
Loving someone that gets you,
Is the ultimate love.

But then,
As luck would have it,
We'd become too
Dependent...

He became the repairer
Of all my damage,
And
That burden was too much
Yet,
I still wanted to be that for him.

I still needed him to know
That
I wanted to carry that burden for him too.

I wanted to be
The bandage,

The healer of sorts,
But it got too comfortable,
Too easy for us,
To exist
Without conflict...

Oh did I miss it...
"The crazy"
That is...
Our crazy was still,
The love I so wanted to hold on to
Forever...

Because in the absence of conflict
He began to shift.
He,
The one I deemed perfect,
Used my happy,
My support,
My love,
And
My encouragement.

He used me
To be better,
And left me
To wonder
If he valued me...

Still questioning this,
Yet
Once again,

I feared the cycle,
But welcomed him in,
And
Despite my fight,
He felt lucky now.
He continued to
Wipe away the tears
And heal the pain
Of my broken heart,
One after another...

No matter how hard I tried to challenge him,
He'd always find the right touch,
Right words,
Right music,
Right silence,
Or
Right kisses,
Whatever
I needed
To pick up the pieces...

And our crazy didn't seem so bad...

Our crazy seemed way better than being used...

But then,
Moments of comfort
Turned to minutes of laughter
And hours of passion.

But love

Was never mentioned!

We existed in the assumptions
Of love
Hoped for...

And,
I fell,
Well
I felt that love was an understatement
For what he'd shown me,
So
I started to believe again.

And with that
He still promised
-Without words-
To love me,
Need me,
And
Heal me,
Again.
And meant it...

I tried not to panic!

I just
Allowed him to apply new bandages
To wounds
He thinks he mended.

Like

The scab of a love I once held
For an old friend.

So easily
I questioned
Can it really be Happily Ever After?
Right now?
He and I?

Thoughts flooded my brain,
Overthinking...

Only to come to my senses
One day,
And realize that happily ever after
Could never be,
For obvious reasons...

Yet,
Because
When I looked at him
And saw love,
-Through lust-
In shades of
Blush,
And cerise,
I saw my happy ending.

I knew
I was stuck in a loop
Of
Temporary insanity...

Stuck
On the hope of longevity
But,
There was too much history.

I knew
That we
Could never equate to destiny.

Reality check!

I'm a sceptic,
I went right back to square one,
Ashamed...

But then,
Like a pair of new heels
I broke my heart in,
To the reality that
I would not be
Eligible
For happy
Ever again...

And,
Through wine stained sheets,
Blouses,
And canvas
I painted away
His memory...

Only for him to return
Over and Over,
And over,
Again,
In my dreams,
Consuming my present
Until,
I gave my hand,
To a new friend...

Can't believe
How easily
I let him in.

I saw clearly
My future
In terracotta,
Upbeat.

We were so easy,
It was no longer hard to breathe.

It was,
Now trouble-free
For me
To choose a new color,
A new shade of happy.

I had him to thank,
Because
After my heart stopped bleeding
He patched me up,

Over and over,
No matter how I strayed
Or hoped
That the previous lover,
Would love me again.

One day.

He,
The current,
Was the moment
When
"In love"
Started to make sense...

And over time
I began to notice
That the way he loved on me
Was more than
Anything
I'd ever experienced...

But again,
As no surprise to me,
No matter how perfect he'd be
My heart
Wouldn't let go of the past.

As usual,
Past paradise
Kept me
Caught

In an emotional cycle,
Intertwined,
On an emotional loop,
Wanting him more
Than hoping for better.

So,

Because I couldn't see
That
The love I had currently
Was a beautiful thing,
I focused
On trying to find a way to destroy the memory,
Of the one I'd lost.

He still was just as real as air to me.

And,
Even though he didn't exist in my present,
He was still very tangible for me...

I figured,
One last attempt.

I was
Sick and twisted,
So
I decided to test him...

I questioned,
Whether he'd come back

And rescue me,
So
I pushed him away,
Stupidly,
In hopes that he'd return
To me.

I sought the attention.

I hoped that if
He heard me crying
He'd reached out to me
And
Finally admit
That living life without me
Was not easy.

He never did...

But
I saw his pain.

I fed off of it...

I used it to
Move on.

And,
Because the current
Was so perfect,
I became conflicted
Dazed and confused.

My mind was consumed with the past.

My heart
Desired the love the present fed...

And with heart and mind
Not alike,
I tore and lit photos.
I,
Torched his memory.

It kept me warm,
Burning in the fire place at night.

I physically
Eliminated all memories of him.
With prayer and meditation
I'd never see
Cross paths
Or encounter him.

All because he failed to acknowledge,
He was lifeless,
In my absence.

It devastated me
To see him move on
To see him try to exist
Without me.

It hurt me deeply.

I knew
Moving on from him
Would be the most challenging thing
I had to overcome.

It was ironic to me.
Assuming a role in life without him in it...

It wasn't what I predicted,
Or wanted.

I was undoubtedly stuck,
In a troubling dilemma.

Forced to accept,
That
I was at the point of no return with him,
While hoping to be saved
By him.

I didn't allow anyone else in.

I was unwilling to admit
That.

The man who supported me,
Loved me through pain,
Accepted my reluctance,
And
Understood my justification,
Was "The One".

He was my friend and love mate.
I should have basked
In his healing power,
But I ran...

Not literally though.

I kept him in the safe space.
Away from the potential harm
So I embraced everyone but.

And he
Shared in my journey.

He listened to me
Intently...

So,
Regardless to the burden of proof,
I
Welcomed the new.

I,
Opened my heart up to all
But the one I knew was true.

After all
Why choose?
When I can have it all.

They fulfilled me in so many ways.

Kept me hot
In places I didn't know they could ignite.
And he delighted in my pleasure.
He took pride in my honesty
And loved every inch of me,
Silently...

I didn't know what to do.

Again
Torn now,
I liked the way it felt,
To have it all.
Him and them.

But,
Some part of me
Still
Missed you...

The past still consumed...

I was done now.

Tired of thinking about
What was
So,
I gave in
To chestnut.

A lovely new shade.

A new him.
And my heart beat
At the same pace,
To the beat
Your drums made,
But
The melody
Definitely changed...

He and I were so in tune
Changing the color in sight.

I now was in love.

I saw shades of gules,
And it was nice,
To see something other than you...

I made him the story I longed for.

I gave him
The love
You once yearned for.

And my heart smiled
Again.

No bad blood
Just happy dreams.

I see clouds traveling
Far away from the shadows,

And all it took
Was for me to focus
On better now...

I continued
To pursue my life's dreams
With all the support he gave me.

All that I could ever ask for,
My reality,
He's seen,
Yet ironically,
She,
Me,
I,
Was confused
Emotionally...

Because
All that life is
Makes little sense,
But feels,
Like anything is possible.

I wanted you so bad
I never envisioned life
In this scope,
So,
I tried to focus
On the present
But
I still write for you...

No matter what I want
Or hoped for,
Life's journey varies
From my dreams
So,
I ripped out the pages.
Book incomplete...

Heart and mind separated.
Consumed with questions...

Where to now?

No direction.

I literally just got out of the shadows.
My peace stirred.

In love I thought I was
But
My heart says you,
My mind says him,
My soul wants and needs
To be free
To love again so,
I
Mentally paused,
For a good reason...

I made time
To think straight.

I made time
To see life
In landscape…

I was engulfed in a garden,
And I have been here
All season.

Still standing motionless,
Replaying memories
In the space where
I watched our love bloom,
Orchids,
Lillies,
Tulips,
My favorite flowers sprung,
Solidifying that
Our love,
Was the greatest…

I had a green thumb but
The fall came,
Leaves flew from the trees,
My direction now obscured.

Should I
Follow the leaves?

My mind says
To my heart,
Or,

Should my soul,
Continue to sing
Loveless tunes?

Or,
Should I continue
To exist in the memory of what was,
Amidst the fallen,
Surrounded by weeds
And
Leafless trees?

How ironic,
Autumn,
-My favorite time of year-
Yet,
My heart sings a different song.
My ears consumed with the blues,
Because I miss him so.

Even breathing consists of pain.
Chest on fire,
As I wonder why
Your life calls for another...

You're the man
Destined to be mine.
The friend,
That causes butterflies,
At every encounter.

I found love with you.

Created love with you.
The man whose hands held me
When broken...

The man I deemed
The mate for my soul.

The man for whom I now long,
Found love in the arms,
Of another...

Who is she?
Why is she?
Not me...

After all the love he showed me,
I guess it was time
I felt the consequence
Of
No return...

More
Unanswered questions,
And all the memories of what was
Leave me to ponder scenarios,
The what ifs.

But,
Not one of the thoughts that consumed me
Led me to
The answer...

Shades of red,
Yellow,
And orange
In view.

Colors of the sun
Merge
For a better view,
And she smiles
Like she once did before,.

She,
Being me,
Smiles
For the hope of love
In the great outdoors,
Anticipating sunny days
And
Rainbows
But
The showers came...
Cheers
To the rain
Flooding my eyes,
My heart,
My mind,
Blurred lines,
Distorted vision.

I thought I'd drowned...

But,

The sun still spoke to my heart,
And
It sometimes peaks
Through the clouds.
In lighting bolts.

My world now bleak...

What to seek?

Besides rainy days,
Since
I couldn't see sunlight skies.

I had no time
For choices of this kind
So,
I stand proud,
In the midst of it all,
I smile,
In the face of it all,
Then,
Your caress creeps up my back
Subtly,
My eyes closed,
Enjoying it all...

Shades of you,
I see
I can never
Escape.

Why?
Question asked
On repeat,
Why?
Did I ever want to
Leave you...

Protection,
Only answer relevant.

I needed to
Free myself
Of your
Love control,
And
Unconditional hold.

You plagued me.
I couldn't see.

I was blinded by
The passion of you,
The unspoken truth
That you and I were never true.

And the shades of my life,
Now melancholy
And blue,
Acceptance tends to do that to you...

So,
I learned to accept the new,

New love,
New lessons,
New shades.

New scope.

New view...

He was always there,
But he wasn't you.

He waited in line,
Patience is a virtue...

In full focus,
No harm
Or hurt
Shall every come to me
From him.

I have learned
To anticipate your moves
So predictable
You are,
And,
Every time
I encounter you
You hide.

Hide behind malice,
Hurt,
Pain,

And you can't accept
Your part in this...

Shades,
Of Pride,
Of pain,
You see
You're
Consumed with it,
Negative energy,
At the fault of me.

But,
I thank God I learned to see
Through clear eyes.

I said good bye to him.

I parted ways
To dissolve the unhappiness
That consumed you.

Now he
Hates me
Because I got away from it.

Missing me
Because
I gave you peace within.

Consistency,
You gave it,

I yearned for it
But,
I neglected it
And,
I accepted,
My part in it...
Still,
You chose to blame me,
Even though
Nothing
Was at the fault of me.

You,
Held the choices
To your destiny.

You chose.

You made love
Generic.

You were a coward
So,
I refused
To validate you.

No piece of me
Will condone
The
Loveless choices,
Or
Courageless actions

Of you.

And now,
My life,
Void of you (my true love)
Sees hope for a new...

I moved forward,
To a life of love
As a result of lust,
But nonetheless,
A seeded love
A part of me
-And the nameless man-
Was beautiful.

Yet
Despite our plan,
No piece of you
Consumes me...

Destiny?

Perhaps he and I could be
One day,
But first
My soul,
Longs to love endlessly...

The heartbeat inside of me
My baby
And she

-Being me-
A mother
I am now
And not because of you.

He
Gave me life
As his queen...

He and I,
In lust,
Bred life
But she,
Her,
Me,
I,
Was still empty...

Needing to share my story
Needing to bare my soul
To you
My friend.

You stayed
You encouraged
You loved
Me
Through it all.

And now destiny
I hope has its way,
One day.

But instead,
That day
I cringed,
Too much pain,
Not familiar
Broke my concentration,
And then,
I was left to give birth to my baby
And
He was a beauty...

I lived in the moment
Wanting nothing more
Than to hold on to his memory

But how could we?

Time was short
And I was left
To spend my night
Without
The newest part of me.

That
Was the ultimate experience
Of lonely...

So when you came,
Spoke to me,
Loved me,
And

Helped me
Through it all,
I cleared the dark cloud,
I stood tall.

Because of you,
I made it out.

Yet
You (now my greatest friend)
And I,
Suffered most
Because
I
Had no regret
For creating my fondest memory
Of love,
Without consideration to you.

And now,
You and I
Are nothing like we were...

You and I
Are as distant as before,
We met...

And it hurts me to know
That loving you
Is now something
I can't forget.

I need you in my life
My greatest chemistry,
Greatest love,
Greatest memory,
Greatest stories,
Greatest moments,
In life spent with you,
Spent
Hoping for us
And waiting on us to
Get it together.

But,
I guess we need more time,
As our love was just fine
Until I,
Changed things...

I came to accept
I selfishly ignored you.

I acknowledge
That I didn't think of you
Or what you wanted,
Even though
You
Should have shared
Your love for me.
You should have told me
We were more than
Sporadic moments,
Conversations,

Wandering eyes,
And passionate kisses.

Because,
I needed to hear you say it.

I needed,
To believe you wanted
More.

I needed a reason
To trust you,
For I knew,
All that is greater than "the best"
Would be all that you and I could do...

I would have been happiest
To hear you call me
Your most precious,
As
I live
For all the times
You called me "Gorgeous",
I believed it.

And I wanted
To believe in you,
And
Believe in us,
But now,
There is nothing left
But wonder,

Hurt,
And uncertainty…

I dare not see you
I 'd cry my eyes and heart out to you,
Because what I've experienced
In the absence of you,
Is more than enough
To let go of the notion
That my world is better
Without you…

But if I am honest,
You scare me too,
So,
I often wonder
How us,
You and I,
Will ever be
And
If ever
Again…

And,
For some reason still
Hope consumes me.

Love for you,
Unconditional
And
Involuntary,
Which

For me
Keeps faith
In the uncertain...

Life is unpredictable,
That's what we're told
And
That's what I know.

Especially since ,
You haven't given me any reason
To believe otherwise.

So,
My eyes
Know nothing more
Than tears.

My heart
Yearns for nothing less
Than infinite years,
With you...

But then
Shades of red,
From the punctured wound,
In my heart,
Consume my lungs.
They
Are now full,
And
There's nothing left

For me.

There's no way for me
To breathe.

You don't rescue me,
You refuse.
And I,
Unfortunately,
Still call out for you…

I close my eyes,
To anticipate
The reality of what is to come.

Where else would I be?

I spent every waking moment
Loving them,
Teaching them to love,
And hoping
They would love me.

But,
Timing wasn't right,
Yet again,
For me.

So,
He sent you.
(The dealer of love)
He gave me

Another again,
Intentionally to save me...

You
Kissed my lips
And remind me,
That you never left,
And
That you would never
Intentionally
Break me.

But the pain I felt,
All along,
Were uncertainties...

I should have believed in you
More,
I should have known
You would love me
More.

I should have given you
The benefit of the doubt.
But,
I needed to
Give you
The opportunity
To sort things out...

Instead,
I allowed unanswered questions

To fill my chest
And they
Encased my heart,
Now constricted,
It hurt to beat,
So nonetheless,
I anticipated that it would burst
Shattering
Into tiny pieces
Of sadness...

And surely
You
Even though you didn't mean it,
You would be
The cause of the monsoon
Of pain
I knew all too well,
But
Still,
I call you first
To
Control this hell
I thought you caused.

But,
In reality
It was all my fault...

So I had to question
What happened
To make me see,

Only
Shades of pain,
In burgundy,
For agony,
And fear,
Which
Cloud my eyes.

Shades of mahogany,
I see
And
While that sounds like a good thing,
Because
After all,
We know mahogany to be sweet,
Enjoyable and all,
But for me,
I saw
Shades of red so dark
Like
Shades of plum wine
And raisin,
Blocking all things.

I saw
No harmony…

I wanted more for me.
I wanted more
For us.

But then

We failed,
To encounter
The best parts
Of one another.

So,
We were aimlessly drifting
In a world
Where
Uncertainty was not meant to be.

We existed
In a place where
Us
Was for eternity.

So,
How do we go back there?

Can we ever?
Get back there...

I'm left to question
Only
What's left for us now.

Is it
Nothing more than
Broken hearts,
Forgotten memories,
Wine saturated moments,
We dare not relive?

Or even think about?

Where do we go from here?

How can we
Build
Again...

I take seconds,
To think about happy moments,
Minutes,
And hours
When
Love making
Was the movement.

I need us to be
Great,
Happy,
Loving,
Smiling,
Daydreaming,
And
Hoping,
Again...

I love you most,
I always have,
It's something about best friends
Who long to be
Boyfriend and girlfriend
That makes me hopeful

Again,
And make life worthwhile.

Because of you,
I believe
That loving
Is plausible,
Again,
That fairytales
Can be real
For little girls
Who search the world
For hope
To love again,
And then
Reality sets in...

You and I,
Stuck in the bubble of life.

Intertwined with
The consequence for loving
So genuinely
That,
We fear
Hurting one another
So passionately
And,
We can't make it right...

Instead,
We lose track of

The reason we fight,
The reason we love,
The reason we want,
Us
In the first place...

We let go
Of what brought us here,
In this space.

We relinquish the moments,
Minutes,
Hours,
Days,
Nights,
And seconds,
Where
Loving one another
Was never a choice,
Loving one another,
Was always
Bigger than us...

Naturally,
You and I
Came to pass.

You and I,
Loved
So easily.

You and I,

Are something short
Of
Destiny,
Unscripted,
Unrehearsed,
We,
Find one another
Again
So
Effortlessly...

But like life,
Choices,
To you from me,
Choices,
Broke our understanding,
Choices,
Took us to spaces
Where
We wait to see,
If our love was
Genuine enough,
For us to get back
To
The moments,
Minutes,
Hours,
Days,
Nights,
And seconds
Where
Loving one another

Was never a choice.

Loving one another
Was
Bigger than us...

But,
I still
Can't quite make sense of it,
Can't believe we
Were penciled in
To eternity.

Still,
Parts of us
Fear the opportunity,
We hesitate at the purity,
So we dance around the possibilities,
We run away just to see,
If we'd be brought back together again...

We,
Can't quite understand
How we got chosen,
So we haven't learned
That when fate speaks,
We need to listen
And,
Hone in
To the faint whispers providing direction,
To the mirrors of our reflections,
Dancing in the greatest space,

That few lovers have the pleasure to share.

You and I,
Need to learn to just be.

And,
Adhere to the instruction.

We can't fear the repercussions,
We must
Smile at the unknown
And,
Embrace every storm
Of our once perfect world...

We can't walk away
In the wrong direction,
And then
Walk back to us,
With hesitation.

Yet
Despite it all,
I delight in optimism.

Not knowing that
Our views would collide
And
Reality aside,
What we expected
Was not what we'd find.

And it happened so quickly.

Where to now?

How do we exist now?

Still no answer comes to mind...

Stuck standing still,
Backs against the wall
Only a few inches apart
But,
We'd dare not peer to the side...

For
If we had
Only blank stares
Would meet our eyes
In darkness...

But I did see
I saw you look away from me
With intent to keep
Your focus
Elsewhere...

Shame filled my heart.

I was forced to cry
Tears of rejection,
Loneliness,
And sadness,

As
I was now
Friendless…

A reality I didn't expect
Because
You were more,
You were the greatest love
I'd ever known.

We shared
A connection
Only God
Could condone.

We were
Heavenly,
And
It's a tragedy
That
Friendship so pure,
And love
So beautiful,
Yet insecure,
May never again
Be…

Shades of crimson
Meet my soul.

Bruised and broken,
While my spirit

On fire for
The world I once knew...

Like ember to ashes
We disperse,
Leaving traces of perfection
In the glow of emptiness...

SHADES OF RED:

REBUILDING

I put the pieces together after you.

I made sure
To be hopeful about a love,
Because
There had to be better
To come,
Whether out of pain
So,
I remain
Patience.

I wait.

I put the pieces
Of her,
(Me)
Together,
Brick by brick,
Stone by stone,
And
I am still nowhere near finished.

Can you imagine,
Aligning chipped segments?

It's like trying to construct
A puzzle with a million pieces.

It feels
Completely impossible
In the moment,

So,
Imagine my frustration,
And
Sympathize with my dedication,
Empathize
For the love I have for her (me).

An unwavering desire
To create a reflection
Of greatness...

I persevere.

Through the pain,
I see clearly,
I make sense of it,
I find a way
For you to still be apart of me
And I
Can exist
Even in our darkest memories.

I learned
That losing you
Didn't mean letting you go.

I learned,
That love is one of those emotions
You have to understand,
In order to control.

I allowed myself to accept the situation.

I grew to understand your purpose.

I saw clearer.

Now we exist
As best we can,
You 1,082 miles away,
And I
A wondering soul…

I found peace
In what is.

I found the love
I knew you couldn't give,
In me.

Simply stated,
I replaced you
With me,
And now life
Is better than
Any classic movie.

Love is greater than
Loving hopelessly.

And I am great,
Because I believe in me.

Instead of anger,

I find gratitude
In all the hard lessons
I encountered
While loving you.

So,
Now I say
Thank you.

I am grateful to you
That I can be open to
Encountering
The best version of me,
And an even greater version
Of you...

Those shades of fire
Turned soft
Cerise,
Rose,
And
Blush.

I was able to dance in daffodils.

I looked forward to
Watching clouds travel across the sky.

Now,
I am happy with how time
Passes by...

I found its place
In my world,
It being time.

It
Was no longer
Flying by.

I live
In every moment,
Minute,
And second of the breeze.

Time was no longer against me.

It stood still
So that I could breathe.

Effortlessly.

But
Just as I got the courage
To speak on past love,
You called to me.

You,
Essentially beckoned me,
And I was
Grateful,
You were right on time,
And we've been perfect
Ever since...

I never imagined such bliss.
Such a real easy love...

I tried to recall
An unhappy memory,
But I remembered
The first day
Like
It was yesterday
And I saw shades
Of cherry and ruby.

You and I
Locked eyes,
It felt
Heavenly.

From that moment
I knew,
We'd be
Living
In a world
Where rules
And dreams
Meet...

Long talks,
Quiet stares,
Effortless smiles,
And
Sentences ended,

Without a need for words.

Like air.

Easy and free.

We'd agree to all things.

You were a lover
I'd have
For eternity.

Or at least
That's the way it seemed…

Of all the years of memories,
The moments of love,
Passion
You shaded me
Blush,
Blinded by your smile,
Your trust,
Your tone,
Your honesty,
And genuine glow.

I love
The sight of you,
And it was good,
We are good,
Easy,
Carefree,

No rules,
Just peace
And
The freedom to be,
In an imperfect world
Where
Our pain
Kept us scorn.

And
Although this,
Us ,
We,
Seemed perfect,
We
Had our fair share of torment.

But,
Our desire to be,
Outweighed the strife.

After all the confusion,
Mystery and fear,

We became the greatest love
To ever appear,
On earth...

SHADES OF RED:
THE CONCLUSION

I realized that in this life I have loved men who have been broken and men whom, I believed, identified with, and accepted, similar broken parts of me. It was those men, I chose to love hard. But often loved wrong.

However, regardless to the way the lesson unfolded, I've learned, oh God I've learned, so much from each one. Each lesson of love taught me to be more open, love freer, and find comfort in vulnerability.

Before these lovers, I believed that vulnerability was something that kept us "unhappy".

I grew up in a household with a strong women. My mother very rarely, if ever, displayed vulnerability, so, I can honestly count on one hand the amount of times I've seen my mother cry in 34 years. Therefore, as an adult woman, vulnerability is one of my greatest challenges. And because I've never had an example, I was never taught that vulnerability is natural and necessary.

But through my journey, I've come to understand that in actuality, it's a woman's ability to hold the present accountable for the past inadequacies, that keeps her stuck in a cycle of unhealthy love. NOT her willingness to show vulnerability.

I like many, got stuck in the cycle of unhealthy attachments to superficial love. That which hindered my ability to recognize healthy love.

I got stuck in this cycle for years!

Unfortunately, I lost a great love due to this cycle of fear.

It took consistently being loved, genuinely, by a man who accepted me, and everything I was, without desire to change or correct me, for me to see clear.

A man who valued every part of my stubbornness and sometimes lack of consideration. Because while I have never been someone who was selfish, I was someone who was certain of what I wanted,

and what I needed. And I wouldn't budge until I
got just that.

Shocked me though the day I actually found it (a
healthy love). Because it took me some time to
realize that it was everything I wanted, it just
didn't look quite the way I had expected it to.

Matter of fact, it didn't look at all like I desired,
so I was reluctant.

I had to admit, however, that it felt amazing! And
when I let him in, he grounded me and gave me a
sense of peace that I had not otherwise known.

I didn't have to be scared. I didn't have to worry.
I was carefree. He loved me without reservation.
And I, blinded by my insecurities, unconsciously
took advantage of it.

In hindsight, I'd apologize a million times for that
now, but I think it may be too late.

Either way, we were great. He and I loved
effortlessly and I consider myself lucky just to
experience that kind of love at all. Some of us
don't get the pleasure, so, I consider myself
privileged to know the peace of sharing space and
time with another effortlessly.

And, I graciously look forward to either encountering that love again, better than it was before, or being just as free to love and feel safe with someone new.

I hope to be comfortable creating room, for that kind of love to manifest in my future.

Life is not always picture perfect, so when you can look back on the hardest moments of your life, and appreciate the time someone else invested in your happiness, what you remember as pain, is really monumental memories, of small victories.

I get it now, so I want you to know that I see you. I love you. I thank you for loving me through the most difficult time in my life. Thank you for not judging the person I've become. Thank you for understanding my love. Thank you for loving me no matter what.

Thank you for trusting me with your heart.

Thank you for sharing countless moments, minutes, hours, days, weeks, months and years loving me. Thank you for accepting me. Thank you for seeing me and smiling. Nothing has ever felt more right in my life, and I can only hope that we both again get to share this same space, with someone just as deserving.

I'll love you forever. xx